GW01112321

PiXZ PEOPLE
Little Books of Great Lives

WINSTON CHURCHILL

RODNEY LEGG

First published in Great Britain in 2011
Copyright text © 2011 Rodney Legg

Cover photographs include: *Winston Churchill with the Earl of Birkenhead (bottom left, front), General Sir Alan Brooke and General Sir Bernard Montgomery (back)*.

All rights reserved. No part of this publication may be reproduced, stored in a retrieval system, or transmitted in any form or by any means without the prior permission of the copyright holder.

British Library Cataloguing-in-Publication Data
A CIP record for this title is available from the British Library

ISBN 978 0 85710 053 5

PiXZ Books
Halsgrove House, Ryelands Business Park,
Bagley Road, Wellington, Somerset TA21 9PZ
Tel: 01823 653777
Fax: 01823 216796
email: sales@halsgrove.com

An imprint of Halstar Ltd, part of the Halsgrove group of companies
Information on all Halsgrove titles is available at: www.halsgrove.com

Printed and bound in China by Toppan Leefung Printing Ltd

The bulldog look

CONTENTS

CHILDHOOD AND YOUTH ... 4
GUNG-HO HEROISM ... 12
YOUNG PARLIAMENTARIAN ... 18
HOME SECRETARY ... 21
FIRST LORD OF THE ADMIRALTY ... 23
COLONEL CHURCHILL ... 26
COLONIAL SECRETARY ... 28
CHANCELLOR OF THE EXCHEQUER ... 29
THE WILDERNESS YEARS ... 31
WARTIME PRIME MINISTER ... 34
LEADER OF THE OPPOSITION ... 59
PRIME MINISTER ONCE AGAIN ... 60
RETIRED STATESMAN ... 62
STATE FUNERAL ... 64

'Never in the field of human conflict was so much owed by so many to so few.'
Winston to Parliament, 20 August 1940

CHILDHOOD AND YOUTH

1874

Date: 30 November at 01.30 hours.
Name: Winston Leonard Spencer-Churchill.
Place: Blenheim Palace, Oxfordshire.
Delivery: Prematurely, by Dr Frederic Taylor from nearby Woodstock.
Hair colour: Red.
Father: Lord Randolph Churchill MP (Member for Woodstock, born third son of John Spencer Churchill, 7th Duke of Marlborough, and Frances Stewart [known as Duchess Fanny], daughter of the 3rd Marquess of Londonderry).
Mother: 20-year-old Jennie Jerome, daughter of Mr and Mrs Leonard Jerome, stockbroker and a founder of the American Jockey Club, from New York City.
Their meeting: At a dance aboard HMS *Ariadne*, off Cowes, hosted by the Prince and Princess of Wales on 12 August 1873. They married on 15 April 1874 at the British Embassy in Paris.

Ancestry: As well as direct connection with John Churchill, 1st Duke of Marlborough and the hero of the Battle of Blenheim (from roots in Dorset and Wiltshire) Winston's Spencer family link went back 15 generations in a male line to Sir John Spencer of Althorp (knighted by Henry VIII) from Warwickshire sheep-farming stock.

1877 Winston's nursery was Little Lodge, beside the Viceroy's Lodge, in Dublin. Randolph Churchill moved there in January as private secretary to his father, the Duke of Marlborough, who Disraeli appointed Viceroy of Ireland. The nanny, Mrs Elizabeth Everest - a large lady - was known as 'Woom' or 'Woomany'. Winston played with tin soldiers on the floor. He remembered his parents being dressed to ride with hounds.

Blenheim Palace was Winston's birthplace in 1874

> 'My mother always seemed to me a fairy princess: a radiant being possessed of limitless riches and power. She shone with me like the Evening Star. I loved her dearly - but at a distance.' Winston's reflections on his mother

To Edward Vincent (Lord D'Abernon), Jennie Churchill was 'More of the panther than of the woman in her look, but with a cultivated intelligence unknown to the jungle.' Jennie's letters from their three years in Ireland include mentions of Winston being 'such a darling'. He asked for 'an ephelant [elephant]' and learnt to sing the song *We will all go hunting today*. Winston recalled riflemen in Phoenix Park, fire destroying the Royal Theatre, and 'the old Duke, the formidable grandpapa' unveiling Gough's statue. His baby brother John ('Jack') was born in Dublin on 4 February 1880. Next month they returned to Blenheim for Randolph to defend his family seat in the general election.

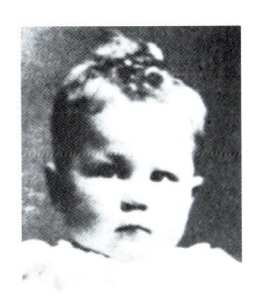

'All babies look like me'

1881 Winston wrote his first letter that has been preserved on 4 January, from Blenheim to his Mamma in London, to thank her for Christmas presents.

> 'Soldiers and Flags and Castle they are so nice it was so kind of you and dear Papa . . .' Winston's first 'thank you' letter

No. 29 St James's Place, Westminster, became the Churchill home for the next five years.

1882-1883 That happy childhood ended in November with entry to St George's School, Ascot, and his first encounter with stern disciplinarian headmaster Revd. H. W. Sneyd-Kynnersley. He had to memorise five states of the Latin word 'mensa' (in three of which the word remained the same). A confused Winston asked what it meant and was threatened with a beating. Bottom of the class, he was described as a 'pickle', being 'very feeble' with 'spelling about as bad as could be'. Only history was 'very good'. Though there were improvements he remained 'troublesome'. 'He has no ambition,' Kynnersley concluded.

The 7th Duke of Marlborough died on 5 July 1883. He was succeeded by Lord Randolph's brother, the Marquess of Blandford, as the 8th Duke. Lady Blandford had divorced the Marquess that February on the grounds of his adultery with Lady Aylesford. Randolph, who toured Europe, was seriously ill with inflammation of the brain membrane.

1884 Lord Randolph recovered to give an acclaimed speech in Blackpool describing William Ewart Gladstone's transatlantic voyage in which Poet Laureate Alfred Tennyson 'adorns a suite and receives a peerage as his reward, and the incidents of the voyage are luncheon with the Emperor of Russia and tea with the Queen of Denmark'. He then announced he was taking 'Tory democracy' into the radical heartland by challenging the Liberal hierarchy in the central division of Birmingham. Mrs Kynnersley visited Birmingham and said 'they were betting two to one that Papa [Randolph] would get in'.

Then Winston was suddenly 'withdrawn' from St George's School (apparently after Mrs Everest saw evidence of a recent birching). He was sent to a smaller and more relaxed institution run by the Misses Thomson at 29-30 Brunswick Road, Hove, Sussex. Randolph meanwhile seized chairmanship of the National Union of Conservative Associations.

1885 In the winter of 1884-85, Randolph went on a four month tour of India, having been earmarked as its Secretary of State by Lord Salisbury. Winston was constantly being asked for his father's signature to stick into autograph books.

In Brighton, the driver of the electric railway predicted 'Lord R. Churchill would be Prime Minister'. On returning from a joint visit to the United States, Lord and Lady Randolph moved into 2 Connaught Place, London W2. Winston's holiday, by contrast, was to Chesterfield Lodge, Cromer, with a 'strict and stiff' governess. The year ended with Randolph failing to take Birmingham but finding an 'admirer' who stepped aside to give him the safe seat of South Kensington.

1886 'Winnie' became dangerously ill with pneumonia in March. He was nursed through the crisis (temperature 104.3 degrees Fahrenheit) by Dr Robson Roose. Normal boyhood returned in July with requests for money.

His parents - Jennie and Lord Randolph Churchill

> *'I am very sorry to say that I am bankrupt and a little cash will be welcome.'*
> *Winston to his parents*

Having taken months to recover, Winston proved in November that he was back on form. He beat doctor's son Bertie Roose, in gymnastics, by three marks. During the year Randolph coined the famous phrase that summed-up the principal obstacle to Irish Home Rule: 'Ulster will fight, and Ulster will be right.'

Gladstone was brought down and Lord Salisbury's consequent victory (316 Conservatives supported by 78 Liberal Unionists) was credited to Lord Randolph. In his triumph he became Leader of the House of Commons and Chancellor of the Exchequer but threw it all away with a maverick pro-German, anti-Russian speech in Dartford followed by an intemperate letter which the Prime Minister accepted as his resignation on realising it was about to appear in The *Times*. A glittering career could go no further. Friends and family alike were devastated and Winston felt the blow for the rest of his life.

Winston asked his father whether he had been to Harrow; Eton was the answer, and had been for the previous five paternal predecessors. Christmas was spent at Blenheim but Randolph stayed in St Petersburg.

1888 In January the family moved to No. 46 Grosvenor Square, Mayfair. Sir George Wombwell, who rode in the Charge of the Light Brigade, took Winston and Jack to a Drury Lane pantomime. Lady Randolph found Winston 'a handful' because of the effect his 'bad language' had on Jack. Winston resumed cramming in Hove for the Harrow entrance examination. He 'scraped through it' and entered Harrow on 17 April. Winston protested at the abuse of his name in school lists and demanded being known as he would style himself for his entire life.

Jennie Churchill with sons Jack (aged 9) and Winston (14) in 1889

1887 Winston was to have gone to Winchester but in the autumn - on advice from brother-in-law Edward Marjoribanks - Lord Randolph entered his name for public school at Harrow.

> *'I never write myself Spencer Churchill, but always Winston S. Churchill.'*
> Winston's protestation at Harrow

He became an enthusiastic member of the School Rifle Corps. In July he won a prize for reciting 1,200 lines of Macaulay. The summer holiday was to the Isle of Wight home of Mrs Everest's sister at 2 Verona Cottages, Ventnor. In November, Gettysburg veteran Colonel Gouraud introduced the phonograph to Harrow. Winston sang 'John Brown's body lies a mould'ring in the grave'.

1889 Lord Randolph disappointed Winston in July by failing to turn up on Speech Day - he never visited Harrow - though he was sent a bicycle in consolation. Winston was put in the school's Army Class and groomed for Sandhurst. Thanks to remedial classes held by Mr Somervell, he acquired lasting admiration for the English language.

1890 Lord Randolph took a small country house at Banstead, near Newmarket, for the summer, on emerging as a winning owner and being elected to the Jockey Club. Lady Randolph chided Winston for working 'in a fitful inharmonious way' and his preliminary examination for the Royal Military College was postponed from June to 10 December. The previous night Winston pulled out a map at random to practice drawing it from memory. Sitting the geography test he found the first question was about that very map of New Zealand.

For his essay he was offered another winner - the American Civil War - and overall he was one of only 12 (out of 29 candidates from Harrow) to pass in all subjects despite being from the lowest form.

> *'I have received very many congratulations from scores of boys and many masters.'*
> Winston on reactions to examination results

1891 Winston established the 'Den' at Banstead as a fighting fort. Exploits at Harrow included smashing windows at a derelict factory, causing 'a deuce of a row', for which he was swished. Lord Randolph, suffering a brain disorder, went to South Africa for climatic relief.

Lady Randolph, still a beauty, flitted about high society with Count Kinsky being among her 'competitive band of handsome young admirers' as grandson Randolph Churchill described them in his biography. Her piano playing entranced them. Kinsky drove Winston in his phaeton to see a fireworks display at Crystal Palace for the visiting German Emperor. Laura Caroline, Lady Wilton, stood in as Winston's 'deputy mother'.

> *'I feel less keen about the Army every day. I think the Church would suit me better.'*
> Winston's thoughts on his future

Years later, son Randolph mused how different things might have been if Winston had chosen the Church rather than the Army. Because his father inevitably crossed the aisles he might have been Pope rather than Prime Minister in 1940. Winston was sent to France for Christmas to learn the language.

1892 The remainder of the family gathered over the New Year at Canford Manor, Dorset, with Lord Randolph sporting what Jack described as 'a horrid beard so ragged'. Winston won the sword-fencing cup at Harrow in March and then the Public Schools Fencing Championship at Aldershot. In the Further Entrance Examination at Sandhurst he came a middling 390th out of 693 candidates. He had to try again in November.

1893 Winston heard in January that he had come 203rd out of the 664 would-be Sandhurst entrants. This again was failure. Arrangements were made for him to return to see Captain Walter James with a view to special cramming but the plan was overtaken by events. While staying at Branksome Dene - seaside home of aunt Cornelia, Lady Wimborne, between Bournemouth and Canford Cliffs - Winston played hide-and-seek with younger brother Jack and a 14-year-old cousin. As they closed in on him, Winston crossed a rustic bridge in a chine, and jumped sideways over the balustrade. Misjudging the leap into a pine-tree he tumbled '29 feet on to hard ground'.

Three days later a comatose Winston regained consciousness. Serious internal injuries included a ruptured kidney. He was kept in bed for two months in Lord and Lady Wimborne's main home at Canford Manor near Wimborne.

On 21 April, as the guest of Dublin MP Edward Carson,

Winston enjoyed his first Parliamentary treat - dinner and attendance at the second reading of the Home Rule Bill. Good news came from Sandhurst in August. It was third time lucky (95th out of 389). Though inadequate for the infantry Winston was offered a cavalry cadetship. To celebrate he went on a Swiss walking tour. A naked swim with a boy in the lake at Lucerne nearly came to grief when a breeze halted their return to the boat. Death, they sensed, was with them a mile offshore.

Despite Winston's persistence and progress in the military, Lord Randolph was infuriated that his son's 'slovenly happy-go-lucky harum scarum style of work' had resulted in 'an extra charge of some £200 per year'. To his relief, Winston was then upgraded to the infantry. 'Sandhurst has done wonders for him,' Papa later conceded.

1894 In the spring Winston was adopted by the 'magnificently dressed' Colonel John Palmer Brabazon from County Mayo who commanded the 4th Hussars at Aldershot. A dashing veteran of the African campaigns he delighted in young company.

Winston wanted to enter the cavalry after all. Strong-willed, he led an act of civil unrest, throwing down barricades erected to appease 'prowling prudes', by separating drinkers in the bars of the Empire Theatre, Leicester Square, from an adjoining promenade where ladies paraded.

The 8th Duke of Marlborough, who had been estranged from Randolph for years, died suddenly in November and was succeeded by Lord Blandford (Winston's cousin Sunny). Winston could now return to Blenheim for Christmas. Lord Randolph's behaviour and speech deteriorated as he edged into the 'mental paralysis' that was destroying his life. Confused, he thought that Winston had gone to Eton rather than Harrow. Public addresses became incoherent. *Hansard* stenographers charitably invented words for a speech that he might have given. Prime Minister Lord Rosebery wrote: 'There was no curtain, no retirement, he died by inches in public.'

Against medical advice, Lord and Lady Randolph sailed for the United States in June and continued across the Pacific, to Japan and India. Forced to cut short the tour in Madras, they came back to London on Christmas Eve.

GUNG-HO HEROISM

1895 Lord Randolph died on 24 January and was buried in Bladon churchyard, Oxfordshire. Winston also lost his Jerome grandmother and nanny Everest (62) died on 3 July. He missed them all but now, as head of the family, felt a sense of freedom. Sandhurst ended well. He passed out 20th (in a class of 130) and was commissioned to join the 4th Hussars. A £100 bank loan secured polo ponies.

Scandals soon surrounded the games. In one a substituted horse, ridden by Winston, came third in a Challenge Cup steeplechase.

Winston and Reggie Barnes audaciously obtained Brabazon's approval, plus that of Lord Wolseley - Sir Garnet Wolseley of the catch-phrase 'All Sir Garnet' - to go off to Cuba to see how the Spanish were fighting insurgents. Winston sent despatches to the *Daily Graphic* at five guineas a time. He spent his 21st birthday with bullets whistling over his head and joined General Valdez 'in a white and gold uniform on a grey horse' for the battle of La Reforma on 2 December. Embarrassingly for the

Second-Lieutenant Churchill of the 4th Hussars at Sandhurst in February 1895

War Office he was awarded Spain's Red Cross decoration. What surprised him was how few people were being killed.

1896 Winston left Cuba disillusioned with the future that 'undisciplined rabble' held for 'the richest island in the world'.

> *'The rebel victory offers little good either to the world in general or to Cuba in particular. Though the Spanish administration is bad a Cuban Government would be worse, equally corrupt, more capricious, and far less stable.'*
> Winston's verdict on the Cuban conflict

National Hunt Committee adjudication on the previous year's race at Sandhurst declared it void with all participating horses being banned indefinitely. Unconnected allegations of heavy drinking against subaltern Allan Bruce - who was asked to resign - led to the man's father accusing Winston of taking part in 'acts of gross immorality of the Oscar Wilde type' at Sandhurst. Winston issued a writ for libel and received an apology and £500 damages. Dirt sticks, however, and it hurt bitterly when his Harrow's headmaster implored him 'not to let your wild spirits carry you away to any action that may bring dishonour on your school or your name' which was spoken of 'with indignation and contempt'.

Winston yearned to travel to the world's flash-points - such as Crete, the Sudan, Matabeleland or South Africa - as the alternative prospect of going with his 'unfortunate regiment' to India threatened 'useless and unprofitable exile'. He was ordered to sail there, however, in the *Britannia* from Southampton on 11 September. Impatient to land at Bombay, he managed to dislocate his right shoulder by grabbing a dockside tie-ring, causing a chronic weakness for life. The high-point came when Miss Plowden took Winston on an elephant through Hyderabad.

1897 Winston the soldier gave a first-class lecture on musketry in which he was top of the class. Winston the gardener planted more than 50 varieties of standard rose around his bungalow in Bangalore. Winston the sportsman was part of the winning team from the 4th Hussars that won a silver cup in a polo tournament.

For all that, and the inevitable gambling, there was also time for reading history - Macaulay and Gibbon - plus Kipling's latest story, *The Seven Seas* and books on politics and constitutional law. He annotated the *Annual Register* for 1875 with a commentary on contemporary events.

Back in England on leave, on Monday 26 July, Winston delivered his first advertised political speech. Addressing a Conservative Primrose League rally at Claverton Manor, Bath, he jibed that Liberals were 'discredited faddists' who 'are always liberal with other people's money'. Radicals were 'slapdash, wholesale, harum-scarum'. Only the Conservative approach was 'a look-before-you-leap policy' which had given the country 'the strongest Government of modern times'. This 'auspicious debut', commented *The Lady*, 'delighted his audience by the force and mental agility he displayed'.

Hearing of a revolt by Pathan tribesmen in the North-West Frontier, Winston sailed back to India. He talked himself into appointment as a War Correspondent to accompany Lieutenant-General Sir Bindon Blood. Copy was sent to The *Daily Telegraph* in London and the *Pioneer Mail* in Allahabad. Winston could not resist opportunities for participating in what became fierce fighting. By the end of the year he had completed the manuscript for *The Story of the Malakand Field Force* and thought he deserved a medal.

1898 Winston reported direct to the Commander-in-Chief, Sir George White, and stayed with the Viceroy, Lord Elgin, in Calcutta. He agitated to be allowed to go to the next trouble-spot and arrived on the Afghan border in March.

> *'Though I now fear the fighting is all over.'*
> Winston's disappointment on arrival
> at the Khyber Pass

His book was in print but he immediately regretted asking uncle Moreton Frewen to correct the proofs. This had introduced 200 misprints. To the *Athenaeum* magazine it might have been a 'literary phenomenon' but was marred by 'shameful blunders' and 'the punctuation of an idiot or of a schoolboy in the lowest form'. It confirmed him as the 'shallow, ill-educated, slovenly' fellow that others disparaged.

He was anxious to move on and join Kitchener in fighting Dervishes beside the Nile. By a miracle the Prime Minister, Lord Salisbury, not only liked the book but invited Winston to Whitehall in July. Lieutenant Churchill was attached to the 21st Lancers for the Sudan Campaign and ordered to report to Abbasiya Barracks, Cairo. En route he gave a 'rousing' public speech in Bradford which won praise from Liberal philosopher R. B. Haldane. Despatches appeared in the *Morning Post* from August. Venturing on to a ridge, Winston briefed General Sir Horatio Kitchener on the disposition of the Dervishes before the Battle of Omdurman, on 3 September.

Winston then shot seven of them with his pistol in a crucial charge 'five men for certain' - and came through it unscathed. But he described the treatment of the enemy wounded as 'disgraceful'. Thousands were slaughtered after the battle. Bizarre things also happened, such as Lieutenant David Beatty passing in a gunboat and throwing Winston a bottle of champagne, which he waded into the Nile to recover. Once back in London, in October, he was itching to return to India.

1899 India hosted the Inter-Regimental Polo Tournament. Winston duly scored the winning goal for the 4th Hussars, on 24 February, and went on to Calcutta to stay with Lord Curzon - the new Viceroy - for a week. He returned to England, via Cairo, in April to read the proofs of *The River War*, in two volumes, on the recapture of Khartoum. Winston S. Churchill now had a classic to his name.

He decided to leave the Army and enter politics. His first contest, with fellow Conservative James Mawdsley, was for the two seats at Oldham, Lancashire, in July. They lost by about 1,500 votes to Radicals Alfred Emmott and Walter Runciman and blamed their own party for introducing the unpopular Clerical Tithes Bill. Making friends with news moguls Alfred Harmsworth (*Daily Mail*) and Oliver Borthwick (*Morning Post*) paid off on 18 September. Anticipating a Boer War, he signed up to go to South Africa - choosing Borthwick - for £1,000 plus expenses, and copyright of his work.

Winston sailed from Southampton, along with Commander-in-Chief Sir Redvers Buller, in the SS *Dunottar Castle* on 14 October. They arrived in Cape Town at the end of the month. To Winston's relief there was still a war going on. Winston left the ship and went overland by train to the port of East London. There he found a steamer for Durban and arrived before Buller. Winston carried on by train towards Ladysmith but had to evacuate at Estcourt on news that rebels had cut the line. Captain Aylmer Haldane, a friend from India, took him in hand. Theirs was now an armoured train, carrying troops to Frere, where they were ambushed by Free State Commandos. Winston volunteered to recover the engine but came under close enemy fire.

Returning to tend the wounded, he and 55 other men were taken prisoner. Other war correspondents, among those who escaped in the other half of the train - pulled by the engine Winston had freed - bore witness to their colleague's bravery. Winston was taken to Pretoria. The Boers who captured him were commanded by General Louis Botha. Because his heroics had enabled the train to escape, Churchill was refused his freedom, but managed to squeeze through a latrine window with Captain Haldane and a fluent Afrikaans speaker named Brockie.

The trio began to escape into the night on 12 December but Haldane was caught by a sentry as he crossed a wall. Churchill was ahead of him but Brockie was still inside the building. So Churchill alone was out, walking through the streets to a railway line, and managed to climb into an empty coal truck on a train heading across the veldt to Witbank in the Transvaal. There he found the house of colliery manager John Howard who turned out to be British. He hid Winston down a mine-shaft in a stable for pit ponies.

'Churchill escaped,' Reuters reported. There was a £25 reward on his head, dead or alive. On 19 December, after Howard had brought wool dealer Charles Burnham into the conspiracy, Winston was smuggled into a cargo of bales on a railway wagon bound for Portuguese territory at Lourenco Marques. Burnham went with the train and intervened with a timely bribe when the consignment was about to be unhitched and then provided hospitality in the buffet bar after it was boarded by a party of armed Boers. Charles Burnham was reunited with his property in the goods yard and proceeded to spirit Winston to the British Consulate and the steamer *Induna*.

On arrival at Durban on 23 December he was already world news. After a speech to a cheering crowd from the Town Hall steps he took the train to Pietermaritzburg and spent the night as guest of the Governor of Natal, Sir Walter Hely-Hutchinson. The following day he was warmly received by Sir Redvers Buller, at Chieveley.

1900 Buller made Winston a Lieutenant in the South African Light Horse and sent him on 6 January to the front-line on the Tugela River. His brother Jack, on the way to join him as a fellow soldier, was wounded and found himself being nursed by their mother aboard the Anglo-American hospital ship *Maine*. Winston and the action were henceforth inseparable as the first and last British officer allowed to double as a War Correspondent.

Battle names included Spion Kop, Vaal Krantz, Hussar Hill, Potgieter's Ferry and Diamond Hill. There was the relief of Ladysmith, and Winston made an audacious cycle ride through Boer-held Johannesburg to carry a vital message. He was on General Sir Ian Hamilton's march across Orange Free State and the entry into Pretoria. That was his ultimate triumph - personal liberation of prisoners-of-war and ripping down the Boer emblem for replacement by the Union Flag. On 4 July he boarded *Dunottar Castle* to sail home from Cape Town.

His name was back on the Oldham ballot paper for the general election in October. This time all four candidates came within a few hundred votes and the two winners were Emmott (12,947) and Churchill (12,931). Election to Parliament was followed by a lucrative speaking tour across England and (less successfully) to America and Canada. Mark Twain welcomed him to New York. Lecturing in Boston on 17 December, the new MP lunched with his namesake, American novelist Winston Churchill.

'I mean to be Prime Minister of England. It would be a great lark if you were President of the United States at the same time.'
Our Winston to America's Winston Churchill

YOUNG PARLIAMENTARIAN

1901 On 2 February, as Queen Victoria was being buried, Winston sailed in the *Etruria* from New York. He took his seat in Westminster on 14 February and gave his maiden speech four days later on the future of South Africa. 'May I say you will never make a better speech than you made tonight,' said War Secretary St John Brodrick. In the middle of the year Winston lost favour with the Tory establishment on being linked to a group of young dissident diners dubbed 'the Hooligans'. Liberal 'Imperialist' Lord Rosebery agitated for a 'Middle Party'.

1902 In April, Winston led a back-bench rebellion against what he regarded as abuses of martial law in South Africa, and in Britain collective punishments in response to arson attacks at Sandhurst. Tory Government tax on food, to pay for the war, was the last straw.

1903 Winston founded the Free Food League which by July had enrolled 60 Unionist MPs plus numerous dukes and knights. Four ministerial resignations followed in September and Winston decided in his mind that his future probably lay with the Liberal Party.

1904 On 29 March, during the Easter adjournment debate, Prime Minister Balfour left the chamber as Winston stood to speak. He protested that this showed a lack of respect to the House of Commons. Front bench ministers then walked out, followed by most of the Tory back-benchers, leaving Winston virtually alone. Winston said he could no longer support the Government and offered to resign if that was the wish of his constituents. Oldham Conservative Association declined to accept the offer.

In April, Winston spoke during a debate on trades union legislation, from memory, but lost the thread of his speech and sat down bewildered. He never again delivered a major speech without full notes. On 31 May, after the Whitsun recess, Winston entered the chamber, stopped at the bar, and glanced both ways. Proceeding to turn right, he sat down next to Opposition leader David Lloyd George, in his father's old seat. He had crossed the floor. The Liberals found him an alternative constituency in Manchester's Jewish quarter.

1905 On 8 March Winston moved a motion in support of international free trade rather than preferential taxes for food from British Empire suppliers. His debut performance in Manchester Free Trade Hall coincided with the first public demonstration by suffragettes; the city was home to the Pankhurst family who led the cause. Balfour resigned on 4 December and the King called upon the Liberal Sir Henry Campbell-Bannerman to form the next Government. He gave Winston his first ministerial appointment as Under-Secretary of State for the Colonies. Winston chose civil servant Edward 'Eddie' Marsh as his Private Secretary in a Whitehall pairing that would continue through various Government departments for three decades.

1906 The New Year was marked by publication of Winston's two-volume biography of *Lord Randolph Churchill* and the January general election in which he was returned as Liberal member for North-West Manchester with a 'spectacular' 25 per cent majority over his opponent. His Parliamentary year was dominated by the complexities of writing a constitution for a self-governing Transvaal.

There was a lively 'Chinese slavery' row after 50,000 coolies were recruited to work the Rand goldfields. Viscount Milner, ex-High Commissioner of South Africa, admitted sanctioning illegal floggings which the British Government had denied were taking place. Winston, answering a question from Hilaire Belloc MP, called it 'a grave dereliction of public duty'. Churchill thought he acted fairly in steering the House into passing a censure motion in which Milner was not named.

Tories, however, were incensed. They had an ally in King Edward VII who regarded Winston's language as 'violent and objectionable'. It had made 'a painful impression on most people'.

1907 Winston's name was emotionally linked with that of 19-year-old Helen Botha, daughter of 'Boer lion of the Transvaal' Louis Botha, who attended the London Colonial

Conference in April. Winston entered the Privy Council on 1 May. Having gone off as an observer to military manoeuvres in Germany and France, he undertook a five-month tour of Malta, Cyprus, Aden and the East African colonies.

Encouraged by Winston, Botha - in proof of loyalty and reconciliation on behalf of his new nation - presented the priceless uncut Cullinan Diamond (a record 3,025 carats) to the King for his birthday on 9 November.

1908 Campbell-Bannerman was succeeded as Prime Minister by Herbert Asquith who appointed Winston to the Cabinet as President of the Board of Trade. Under an archaic law this required re-election but fickle Manchester rejected him. Then the 'life seat' of Dundee became available.

Politically, Winston quietly adopted several Fabian socialist solutions to labour and welfare problems. Personally, both the energetic minister and his younger brother were in love. Jack married on 4 August.

Winston's turn followed at 2 p.m. on Saturday 12 September. His wedding was to 23-year-old Clementine Hozier - daughter of the late Sir Henry Hozier and Lady Blanche Hozier - in St Margaret's, Westminster, which is the parish church for the House of Commons. Guests included David Lloyd George, who signed the register, but Asquith and most of the Cabinet were on vacation in Scotland. Apart from Winston's bowler-hatted arrival in an Electric Brougham, no known photographs survive of the occasion, according to the Churchill Archives Centre in Cambridge. The reception was held at Lady St Helier's home (79 Harley Street before she moved to 52 Portland Place) and the couple began their honeymoon at Blenheim.

1909 Winston persuaded the Admiralty to bring forward building contracts for 21 warships to alleviate 'a winter of starvation and stress on the Clyde and the Tyne'. Arbitration adjudicators were appointed to reconcile industrial disputes. Legislation was drafted for minimum wages, the introduction of labour exchanges, and national insurance for sickness and unemployment benefits.

To Tories and cartoonists, Winston was a class-traitor,

particularly as he also supported Lloyd George in challenging the House of Lords. In March the Churchills took a lease on No. 33 Eccleston Square, behind Victoria Station, and their first baby, Diana, was born on 11 July. The Kaiser invited Winston to Germany for military manoeuvres in the autumn.

HOME SECRETARY

1910 The Liberals scraped back into power in January (by two seats) and Asquith promoted Winston to the Home Office in February. His speeches, the Prime Minister told him, 'from first to last have reached the high-water mark, and will live in history'. Privately, however, he remarked that 'Winston thinks with his mouth'. In May, though suggesting to the War Office that 'mounted troops' might be deployed to quell rioting miners in the Rhondda Valley, Winston prevented infantry 'with long-range rifles' being used against those looting shops at Tonypandy. The contrary myth, however, went into Welsh folklore.

Winston wavered on the 'Votes for Women' campaign after imprisoned suffragettes went on hunger strike and were force-fed. He personally intervened during their 'Battle of Downing Street' on 22 November to order the arrest of Mrs Cobden-Sanderson.

Watching German manoeuvres with Kaiser Wilhelm II in September 1909

> *'Take that woman away; she is obviously one of the ringleaders.'*
> Winston to policemen, 22 November 1910

Despite strife and strikes, a December general election again returned the Liberals, though it halved their majority.

1911 Affairs of state were seldom dull with Winston in charge. A gang of anarchists led by 'Peter the Painter', having killed three Metropolitan policemen during a botched burglary in Houndsditch, were resisting arrest from a terraced house at 100 Sidney Street, Stepney, on 3 January. The Home Secretary called in troops.

Having commandeered 70 men of the 1st Battalion, the Scots Guards - with a Maxim gun - from the Tower of London he took personal charge of the siege. It ended with the building on fire and two occupants dying in the flames but 'Peter the Painter' vanished.

To Clemmie and Winston, on 28 May, 'Chumbolly' (son Randolph) was born. On 28 June, the Cabinet backed the Winston-Lloyd George solution for removing the House of Lords veto over the Parliament Bill - the threat to create 500 new peers. Playing the military card in August, Winston had HMS *Antrim* sail to Liverpool, as a precaution to keep the ferries going, after Lord Derby claimed 'a revolution was in progress'.

Home Secretary Churchill (centre) between Scots Guards and armed police at the siege of Sidney Street in 1911

Troops were put on stand-by to protect the rail network in the event of a national strike by railwaymen. Though that was settled by Lloyd George, as Chancellor of the Exchequer, four men were shot dead at Llanelli after they ambushed an engine driver and coshed him unconscious. Despite such tensions, Winston pioneered prison reform, encouraging courts to give time for fines to be paid, and generally shorten sentences. Coming home from the golf links in September, after playing with the Prime Minister, Asquith asked Winston if he would like to have the Royal Navy. 'Indeed I would,' said the next First Lord of the Admiralty.

FIRST LORD OF THE ADMIRALTY

1912 Asquith briefed Winston to overcome opposition to his plan for a Naval War Staff. Externally, the perceived threat was from the growing aspirations and might of the Germans. Internally, Irish Home Rule was back as a live issue. Clemmie accompanied Winston when he visited Belfast to speak in the Ulster Hall on 8 February.

Winston in the saddle, hunting from Blenheim, in 1912

They were jeered by a hostile crowd of 10,000 Protestant Ulstermen who lifted the wheels of their car off the ground. Police beat them off. Four battalions of infantry guarded the route from Grand Central Hotel. 'Scowls turned to smiles' when he addressed 5,000 Nationalist Catholics in the Falls Road.

On 9 May, King George V arrived at Weymouth to review the Fleet in Portland Harbour. The following day Winston took the royal party and politicians down a main gun-turret on HMS *Orion*. The King was also given a ride in a submerged submarine.

1913 Winston's prime concern was maintaining British maritime supremacy during the power struggle with Germany. This included airship and seaplane acquisitions for a Naval Air Service. He foresaw both types of craft being turned into armed rather than reconnaissance roles. Having gone up into the air many times, he was on the point of applying for a pilot's certificate, but was dissuaded by a spate of crashes.

Seaborne units were held in reserve for intervention in Ulster. Winston regarded this as an intractable diversion that would eventually require a form of federal government. As a result he was accused of betraying the Irish cause and both sides now regarded him with profound suspicion.

1914 Sir Edward Carson's Ulster Volunteers prepared to fight after successfully gun-running an estimated 35,000 rifles and three million rounds of ammunition in a single night. Faced with a wider threat, however, both sides of the Irish divide set aside their differences to face the international situation. On 23 July, Winston dispersed the Third Fleet to its home ports, and ordered the First (Grand) and Second Fleets to re-group in Portland Harbour. Then he agonised that they might be subject to surprise attack by German motor-torpedo boats and issued secret orders.

Firstly the Second Fleet was dispersed, to training establishments around the country, by 27 July. Secondly the First Fleet was armed and mobilised. After consulting the Prime Minister, Winston ordered it to slip into the Channel, on the evening of 29 July. It steamed 'at high speed, and without lights' through the Straits of Dover and the North Sea to Scapa Flow anchorage in the Orkney Isles. Winston was to send the seminal order at 23.00 hours on Tuesday 4 August 1914 (effective from midnight).

> *'Commence hostilities against Germany.'*
> Winston's order to the Fleet, 4 August 1914

By December, Grand Duke Nicholas of Russia was desperate for a British action against southern Turkey to relieve pressure on his troops in the Caucasus. Earl Kitchener of Khartoum responded with a plan for naval action in the Dardanelles which found a ready supporter in Winston. The stalemate on the Western Front gave added impetus to thoughts that an attack on Turkey could be expanded into landings on the Gallipoli peninsula.

1915 The War Council, on 13 January, not only adopted Winston's plan for an attack in the Dardanelles but widened its objectives. The decision as recorded by the Prime Minister extended to capturing the Turkish capital: 'That the Admiralty should prepare for a naval expedition in February to bombard and take the Gallipoli peninsula with Constantinople as its objective.'

As First Lord of the Admiralty it also happened to be Winston who championed the development of armoured vehicles. He took it upon himself to activate an idea from Lieutenant-Colonel Ernest Dunlop Swinton (who wrote under the pseudonym of Backsight-Forethought) for a mechanised tank after it had been rejected by the War Office. On 20 February he appointed the naval architect Eustace Tennyson-D'Eyncourt to chair an Admiralty Landship Committee.

News from the Dardanelles was initially encouraging as naval gunfire and marine landings silenced the outer ribbon of Turkish guns. Their inner line, however, lay behind eight big minefields. Deadlock resulted. A concerted attempt to force the Straits on 18 March ended with three old battleships sunk and others immobilised. Lord Kitchener intervened to offer ground forces to 'assume the burden' and by mid-May there were 70,000 Allied troops (nearly half from Australia and New Zealand) ashore in an impasse of trench warfare across sandy hills.

The Churchillian crusade in Asia Minor was failing just as Admiral Jackie Fisher, the First Sea Lord, had predicted: 'You are just simply eaten up with the Dardanelles and cannot think of anything else. Damn the Dardanelles! They will be our grave!'

Fisher resigned on 14 May. This and a row over shell shortages on the Western Front precipitated Asquith to negotiate with the Conservatives for a Coalition Government on 19 May. For their part of the deal, the Tories demanded Churchill's scalp and his replacement at the Admiralty by former Prime Minister Arthur Balfour. Winston was consoled by Lord Kitchener, with whom he had so often crossed swords: 'Well, there is one thing at any rate they cannot take from you. The Fleet was ready.'

Winston insisted that the Dardanelles had been 'a legitimate gamble' in which Asquith was 'a co-adventurer'. Although Asquith now offered Winston the choice of a different ministry or a command in France, the King intervened to appoint him Chancellor of the Duchy of Lancaster. This was demotion as the cartoonists saw it. Winston yearned to be on the front-line, so he re-trained as a soldier.

COLONEL CHURCHILL

1916 On New Year's Day, at St Omer, Lieutenant-Colonel Churchill heard he had command of the 6th Battalion, Royal Scots Fusiliers. He arrived at their headquarters with a cart-load of baggage including a bath and boiler. The newly formed unit was to hold trenches beside treeless Bois de Ploegsteert ('Plugstreet Wood' to the Brits) in the far south of Belgium.

Winston was inside Laurence Farm when a German shell crashed through the roof but

Winston with the Marshal of France, Ferdinand Foch, watching British troops enter Lille in October 1918

failed to explode. During the 100 days of his command casualties were relatively light (15 men killed and 123 wounded). On 6 December the management of war took a turn which pleased Winston. Lloyd George replaced Asquith as Prime Minister.

1917 In the House of Commons, in May, Winston urged restraint on the battlefield until United States troops arrived in Europe. After taking over Lloyd George's old job, as Minister of Munitions, he was ruthlessly efficient, putting particular effort into production of aircraft, tanks and poison gas shells.

1918 In the spring, while visiting the front-line, Winston narrowly escaped from under an artillery barrage just before German troops over-ran his headquarters. Eastern Europe was in turmoil from the Russian Revolution and Winston's maverick view was that the Allies should be supporting the Bolsheviks.

German progress on the Western Front reverted to stalemate, followed by a collapse in morale, verging on mutiny. Winston found 275 heavy guns for the newly arrived American artillery. Plans for 1919 assumed the deployment of 3,360,000 United States soldiers.

Winston likened his efforts to the worker 'bees of Hell' storing 'hives with the pure essence of slaughter'. From August the British and French recovered many of the battlefields lost in 1916 and the American sledgehammer - protected by an unprecedented 1,483 aircraft - advanced from St Mihiel in September. By the end of the month the Germans were losing 33,000 men in a day, taken prisoner, on the Hindenburg Line near Cambrai.

They began to sue for peace in October but were told by President Wilson that the prerequisite was total withdrawal from occupied lands. Reparations then became part of the demand, plus surrender of artillery, submarines, surface fleet and railway stock. Their navy was in a state of mutiny - raising the Red Flag over Kiel and Cologne and the Fatherland generally in a state of revolution. The Armistice was signed by German delegates at Compiegne at 05.10 hours on 11 November with hostilities to cease that day at 11.00 hours French time - the eleventh hour of the eleventh day of the eleventh month.

1919 In the first peacetime January Winston was given the joint ministry he craved for in wartime - Secretary of State for War and Air. The Cabinet resisted most of his attempts to send British troops into Russia in support of royalist Whites against revolutionary Reds though he was instrumental in blowing-up two battleships at Kronstadt in the Baltic. He offered a lapidary epigram to the War Memorial Committee. They rejected it but for the author its time would come.

> 'In war, resolution; in defeat, defiance; in victory, magnanimity; in peace, goodwill.'

1920 The Home Rule Bill, postponed for the duration of the war, returned to the agenda. As War Minister, Winston urged the declaration of martial law in Ireland, with a view to summary execution of hostages and prisoners. Police and government officers were being targeted by the Irish Republican Army. In forming the 'Black and Tans' - theoretically policemen, to give the Royal Irish Constabulary para-military support - he ruthlessly matched one terror with another.

> 'The more you shoot, the better I will like you, and I assure you no policeman will get in trouble for shooting any man.'
> Winston to the Black and Tans

The Government of Ireland Act was passed in December.

COLONIAL SECRETARY

1921 In February Winston became Secretary of State for the Colonies. On 6 December, Ireland was partitioned, by the signing of a treaty in which six counties of Ulster remained in the United Kingdom, but the other 26 counties formed an Irish Free State. This was to stay inside the British Empire with a constitutional status similar to Canada. For at least two Republican negotiators - Michael Collins and Erskine Childers - it was a death sentence. The outcome split Sinn Fein and brought about Civil War.

Winston, Clemmie and Colonel T. E. Lawrence on camels in Egypt, 1921

Chartwell, Winston's dream home in Kent, languished as a wilderness when he came across it in 1922

1922 Southern Ireland's General Michael Collins greatly admired Winston, as a message before his assassination shows. It was to 'tell Winston we could not have done it without him'. Winston, Parliament, Liberalism and the Dundee constituency parted company in October.

CHANCELLOR OF THE EXCHEQUER

1924-1929 Ramsay MacDonald formed Britain's first Labour Government in January 1924 but it failed to last the year. Winston stood as Constitutional candidate for the Epping division of Essex when Stanley Baldwin's second Conservative administration was returned at the general election of 20 October 1924. As Baldwin's Chancellor of the Exchequer, Winston sorted out war-debts, trade and tariff duties, and management of the national finances through difficult times.

Against his better judgment he was persuaded by Montague Norman, Governor of the Bank of England, to return Britain to the gold standard. Though earlier acting as a mediator between mine-owners and trades unionists, Winston eagerly became the partisan editor of the *British Gazette* propaganda mouthpiece during the General Strike in 1926.

On Cabinet orders a 'train of departmental officials' had commandeered the offices and works of the *Morning Post* 'on behalf of His Majesty's Government'. Circulation surged from 232,000 on 5 May to 2,209,000 a week later. The strike collapsed and the *Morning Post* resumed publication on 14 May 1926.

Winston presented his last Budget on 29 April 1929. It was soon to be overshadowed by the Wall Street Crash in New York and the return of Ramsay MacDonald to 10 Downing Street.

Winston's closest confidant, Frederick Edwin Smith, 1st Earl of Birkenhead - Secretary of State for India - conversing in a railway carriage, 1928

Behind the wheel - Winston as Chancellor, chauffeuring the President of the Board of Trade, Sir Philip Cunliffe-Lister (1st Earl of Swinton), in 1925

THE WILDERNESS YEARS

1930-1939 Winston's decade of impotence saw him in league with Foreign Office civil servant supremo Robert Vansittart to lobby for British rearmament. Both were horrified as Hitler's Germany edged towards military parity. They were appalled when in June 1935 the Prince of Wales told the British Legion there was 'no more suitable body of men to stretch forth the hand of friendship to the Germans than we ex-Servicemen'. Foreign ministers in both Britain and France colluded to allow Mussolini to occupy Abyssinia.

The great British obsession was with its monarchy. After the death of George V it became clear that the former Prince of Wales - as King Edward VIII - was determined to marry American double divorcee Mrs Wallis Simpson. Winston, the Prince's recent critic, was now the potential royalist. If the Government resigned in protest, Stanley Baldwin feared,

Clemmie and Winston with 13-year-old daughter Mary striding through Westminster to hear King George V's jubilee address to Parliament, 9 May 1935

Winston was liable to stand up for the King and attempt to form an alternative administration. Winston, however, was also opposed to the marriage although he sided with the King's interpretation of the constitution.

> 'What crime has the King committed? Have we not sworn allegiance to him? Are we not bound by that oath? Is he to be condemned unheard? Is he seeking to do anything that is not permitted to the meanest of his subjects?'
> Winston to Alfred Duff Cooper

Winston dined with the King at his Fort Belvedere home on Saturday 4 December 1936. Though under enormous stress he insisted that he had not abdicated. Winston advised him to see a doctor, stay in the country, and to take time before making up his mind. The following day the Cabinet met, exceptionally for a Sunday, to force through an Abdication Bill.

In the constitutional crisis Winston was howled down by fellow Tory back-benchers as the establishment united to remove its King. That took place with dignity and eloquence in a live radio broadcast from Windsor Castle at 10 p.m. on 11 December. Though largely in the King's own words, incorporating phrases from his lawyer Walter Monckton, the moving

Winston's son Randolph marrying the Honourable Pamela Digby from Minterne Magna, Dorset, in the society wedding of 1939

Clemmie and Winston at Moreton, Dorset, for the funeral of Lawrence of Arabia, 21 May 1935

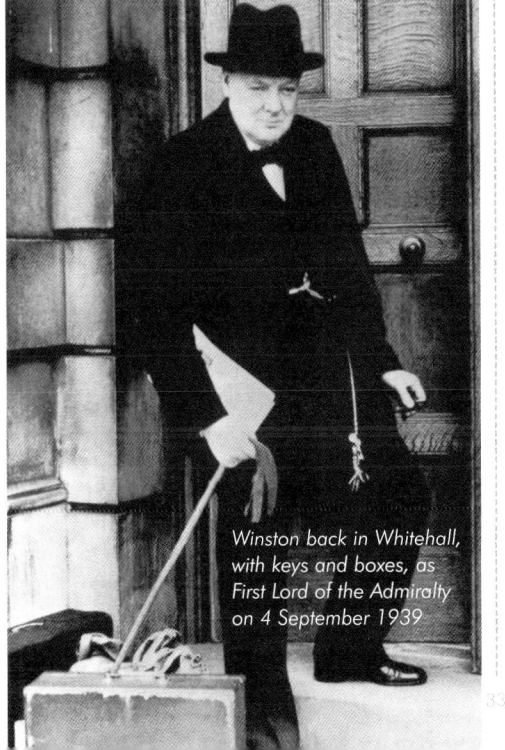

Winston visiting France as First Lord of the Admiralty, 5 November 1939, with Lord Gort VC (Commander-in-Chief, British Expeditionary Force) and Lieutenant-Colonel Sir Henry Royds Pownall (Gort's Chief of Staff)

Winston back in Whitehall, with keys and boxes, as First Lord of the Admiralty on 4 September 1939

speech was 'polished' by Winston. The Duke of York, Edward's younger brother, became King George VI.

Neville Chamberlain, as the next Conservative Prime Minister, had Winston sniping from the back benches against the policy of appeasing Hitler over Czechoslovakia and at their Munich accord.

On 1 September 1939, realising conflict with Germany was unavoidable once German troops moved into Poland, Chamberlain's first move was to invite Winston to join his War

Cabinet. Returned to the service post he lost in the middle of the previous war - First Lord of the Admiralty - Winston set about making memorable broadcasts.

WARTIME PRIME MINISTER

1940   The first months of the 'Phoney War' saw naval activity and losses but little happened on land or in the air. Then the Wehrmacht moved into Scandinavia. The defence of Norway came in May - after the event - and was too late to turn the tide, Winston pointed out.

> *'It is not the slightest use blaming the Allies for not being able to give substantial help and protection to neutral countries if they are held at arms length by the neutral countries until those countries are actually attacked.'*
> Winston on defending Norway

Bulldog look - the wartime Premier

The debate in Parliament on the failed campaign took place on 10 May which turned out to be the day when Hitler invaded Belgium and Holland.   Chamberlain offered to form a coalition National Government but Labour leaders refused to serve under

England alone - Winston inspecting South Coast defences in July 1940

him. He came under vehement criticism from all sides of the chamber.

Lord Halifax was favourite to take over but ruled himself out by saying it was difficult for a peer to run affairs from the Upper House. The Prime Minister broadcast his resignation speech that evening and the King asked Winston to form a Government. Immediately a new dynamism infused Whitehall, though things might have been very different if Hitler had not held back his tanks in France, and the weather obligingly co-operated at the end of the month to enable a 'miracle of deliverance' in which 338,000 soldiers were evacuated from the beaches at Dunkirk.

The Fall of France followed, despite Winston flying twice from Dorset to Paris to bolster collapsing morale, and committing more British troops to resistance further west. A further 100,000 troops did come home to fight another day. From 4 June 1940, however, it was Britain alone, and a resolve encapsulated by Winston with the most memorable speech in the English language.

> 'We shall not flag or flail. We shall fight in France, we shall fight on the seas and oceans, we shall fight with growing confidence and growing strength in the air, we shall defend our island, whatever the cost may be, we shall fight on the beaches, we shall fight on the landing grounds, we shall fight in the fields and in the streets, we shall fight in the hills; we shall never surrender.' Winston to Parliament, 4 June 1940

What followed was the Blitz and the Battle of Britain. On 11 September, Winston was 60 feet underground at Uxbridge, in the bunker commanding No. 11 Group, Fighter Command, as the markers went up for '80+' enemy aircraft in formation over Calais and Boulogne. Air Vice-Marshal Keith Park attempted to round-up three reserve squadrons - all that were available - and on this occasion the attack broke off, with a total of 175 Luftwaffe planes being claimed by the RAF (60 actually, compared with 26 British losses).

Thanks to advance warnings from radar and intercepted German Enigma-encrypted radio traffic secretly decoded at Bletchley Park, Buckinghamshire, the Hurricanes and Spitfires of the RAF maintained air superiority. Hitler was forced to postpone his intended invasion. Winston's Parliamentary speeches captured the national mood of defiance to dictatorship.

War Premier Winston in the Cabinet Room at No.10 Downing Street, September 1940

> 'Let us therefore brace ourselves to our duties, and so bear ourselves that, if the British Empire and its Commonwealth last for a thousand years, men will still say: "This was their finest hour".' Winston to Parliament, 18 June 1940

Winston visiting heavily-bombed Ramsgate, Kent, on 28 August 1940

Posing with a Thompson sub-machinegun, 5 August 1940

For Downing Street use, Winston had his own collection of abbreviations, code-names and phrases:

ATD = Action This Day (stickers were printed for attachment to files and letters)
The Big City = Berlin
A Bomber's Moon = nature's betrayal by brightness (for the once-welcomed Harvest Moon in September and Hunter's Moon in October)
The Colonel = Clementine Churchill (his wife)
Colonel Warden = Churchill himself
Don Q = Don Quixote = President Franklin D. Roosevelt
KBO = Keep Buggering On (his favourite sign-off, which typists were told to ignore)
Operation Smith = Operation Sealion = Operation Seelowe (Hitler's planned invasion)
SP = Sancho Panza = Harry Hopkins (United States Secretary of State)

One of the dangerous weekends with a bombers' moon was that

Prime Minister, King and Queen, amid bomb damage at Buckingham Palace, 13 September 1940

of 16 November, when Churchill stayed at Ditchley Park, Enstone, near Oxford, instead of Chequers. This was the home of Ronnie Tree, the Tory MP for Harborough, Leicestershire, who recalled the visits in his memoirs *When the Moon was High*.

1941 Britain had a powerful but neutral ally. On Sunday 3 August the authors H. V. Morton and Howard Spring, were told they had been chosen to undertake an important journey on behalf of the nation but unaware of where they were going, boarded a special train at Addison Road - a station closed to public use - between Kensington Olympia and Shepherd's Bush. They recognised some of their fellow travellers from the Admiralty, War Office and Whitehall.

Waiting for them on the platform at Wendover in the Chiltern Hills was the Prime Minister, wearing his yachting cap, accompanied by Sir Alexander Cadogan (Permanent Under-Secretary of State for Foreign Affairs), Field-Marshal Sir John Dill, Air Chief Marshal Sir Wilfrid Freeman, Admiral Sir Dudley Pound and Professor Lindemann. By now, having noticed the sleeping-car carriages, the two writers realised they were heading north of the border. Spring sighed on realisation that he had only brought a suit and overcoat. 'You seem to have everything except a kilt,' he told Morton, whose baggage included his Home Guard uniform, dinner jacket and tropical kit.

The train's secret destination on Monday 4 August was Thurso, Scotland's most northerly railway station, on a grey morning with cloud across the hills and fog over the sea. The

Sealing the Atlantic Charter aboard USS Augusta *in Placentia Bay, Newfoundland, August 1941. Standing behind President Roosevelt and Prime Minister Churchill are United States Under Secretary Sumner Welles, Admiral Ernest J. King and Army Chief of Staff General George C. Marshall*

party boarded the *Morning Glory* which decanted them into the destroyer *Orbi*, waiting offshore. She delivered them to HMS *Prince of Wales* - our newest battleship - at anchor in Scapa Flow in the Orkney Isles. American Secretary of State Harry Hopkins, back from Moscow on Sunday, was already on board.

The battleship soon sailed into an Atlantic gale, forcing Churchill to vacate the sumptuous Admiral's quarters over the propellers for relative stability in the sea-cabin above the bridge. Spring, now briefed that he and Morton were there on behalf of the world press (which was to turn sour when they were forbidden to make eye-witness reports) found refuge in the Sick Bay with Churchill's bodyguard, Walter 'Tommy' Thompson. Total radio silence, bringing an inability to send signals, forced Winston into his first rest period of the war.

> 'All this ozone is making me lazy. I used to want to see red boxes all the time. Now I have difficulty in driving myself to two hours' work a day.' Winston at sea in 1941

In the wardroom, his favourite film was Alexander Korda's *Lady Hamilton* starring Vivien Leigh with Laurence Olivier as Lord Nelson (*That Hamilton Woman* it was re-titled for Americans). Churchill's songs of the moment, from both sides of the pond, were Noel Coward's *Mad Dogs and Englishmen* and the lively dance routine *Franklin D. Roosevelt Jones*. Early in the morning of Saturday 9 August they sighted Newfoundland and dropped anchor at 09.00 hours in Placentia Bay beside the cruiser USS *Augusta*. President Roosevelt was waving from the deck.

Winston was impatient to join the Admiral's barge and meet him in person, for the second time. The first had been at a dinner in London in the Great War, when Roosevelt was the Assistant Secretary of the United States Navy. Roosevelt recalled the details but Churchill, unfortunately, had no memory of it, to the President's disappointment. Discussion topics included resisting the Japanese; responses to possible German moves in the Iberian peninsula; Lend-Lease priorities; United States Navy involvement in protecting Atlantic convoys; future prospects for an Operation Round-Up to take the war back across the English Channel. 'Common principles' were affirmed in an Atlantic Charter for 'the final destruction of Nazi tyranny'. Socially, Anglo-American relations had improved with the arrival by flying-boat of Lord Beaverbrook.

HMS *Prince of Wales* weighed anchor at 17.00 hours on 12 August and Winston went aft to wave his cap in farewell to each American warship they passed. As they approached Iceland, the battleship changed course to sail through a convoy of 72 Allied merchant ships, heading for Britain from Halifax, Nova Scotia. Twelve columns, each of a dozen vessels, spread across six miles of sea.

The *Prince of Wales*, at 20 knots, sailed through them twice as the Chief Yeoman flashed the letters 'C-H-U-R-C-H-I-L-L' in Morse code and the Prime Minister gave the V-sign from the bridge. Seamen on the decks cheered and waved. The following day, Churchill boarded a Canadian destroyer for a visit to British and American troops in Reykjavik. Having returned to British waters through a gale, the *Prince of Wales* dropped anchor in Scapa Flow at 09.00 hours on 18 August in bright sunshine. The war proceeded but there were occasional leisure moments in Winston's diary, such as that for 15.00 hours on 4 October:

'Wembley Stadium.'

The next dangerous transatlantic adventure began at noon on 12 December. Wearing a yachting cap, Winston was piped aboard the battleship HMS *Duke of York* off Greenock, with Minister of Supply Max Beaverbrook. On 22 December they anchored in Chesapeake Bay. Winston, Averill Harriman, Air Marshal Portal and Sir Charles Wilson (Churchill's doctor) flew to Washington. On the 27th, in bed at the White House, Winston suffered a minor heart attack, or at least 'coronary insufficiency', his doctor diagnosed. He decided to tell no one.

The following day the British party left Washington for Ottawa. New Year's Eve was spent dining with Canadian Prime Minister Mackenzie King. Churchill recounted how at the time of Dunkirk, Maxime Weygand had gone to the French cabinet and predicted: 'In three weeks England will have her neck wrung like a chicken.' He paused. 'Some chicken, some neck.'

1942 Winston returned to Washington on New Year's Day. From 5 to 9 January, General George Marshall took the British party to Florida in his personal aircraft. Sir Charles Wilson

Soviet Foreign Minister Vyacheslav Molotov (centre) with Winston, British Foreign Secretary Anthony Eden (behind) and Deputy Prime Minister Clement Attlee (smoking) - in the garden of No. 10 Downing Street, 22 May 1942

wrote in his diary: 'The air here is balmy after the bitter cold of Ottawa... the blue ocean is so warm that Winston basks half-submerged in the water like a hippopotamus in a swamp.'

The situation in Malaya had deteriorated and the Australians feared they might be bombed or invaded. Asked whether the Philippines would be forced to surrender to the Japanese, Churchill came out with an unanswerable reply.

> *'That depends on the strength of the forces defending and of forces attacking.'* Winston on being asked if the Philippines would fall

Henceforth, it was made clear to the British delegation at the White House, the war would be run from Washington. Harry Hopkins spelt out to Winston the logistics that were already in hand with the United States committed to increasing aircraft numbers from 45,000 in 1942 to 100,000 in 1943, and its total of tanks from 45,000 to 75,000 in the same period.

On the 15th, preparing to leave from Colgate Creek, beside Harbor Field, Baltimore, Winston was pushed aside by Roosevelt's bodyguard, Mike Reilly, as he wrestled an airport worker with a gun who had been heard muttering: 'I'm going to get that fucking Churchill. I'm going to kill him.'

The return was in Boeing Clipper flying-boat *Berwick* - the largest aircraft in the world - with Winston at the controls for a time, to Bermuda where he was to join the battleship HMS *Duke of York*. Instead, anxious about news of the Japanese advance into Malaya, Churchill persuaded Captain Kelly-Roberts of BOAC to fly him all the way to England. Eighteen hours and 3,000 miles later they nearly came to grief in dense cloud over the Western Approaches.

Making better speed than anticipated they proceeded to within minutes of German air-aircraft guns at Brest. They then found Plymouth Sound, after facing further jeopardy of interception as an enemy aircraft, by British fighters. On the 17th the party was safely in a train to Paddington. President Roosevelt, celebrating his birthday, sent Winston a message on 30 January: 'It is fun to be in the same decade as you.'

Winston was flattered to hear that the new British A22 infantry tank had been renamed the Churchill (a total of 5,640 would be made by General Motors and Vauxhall). Everything was overshadowed, however, by news of the Fall of Singapore when he was staying with the Tree family at Ditchley Park.

The fateful message came to him on 14 February from Field-Marshal Archibald Wavell, in Java, as Allied Supreme Commander South-West Pacific: 'You are of course sole judge of moment when no further results can be gained in Singapore and should instruct [General] Percival accordingly. CIGS [General Sir Alan Brooke] concurs.' The following day Winston told the nation of the fall of Singapore.

> Losing Singapore, said Winston, was
> '. . . *the worst disaster and biggest*
> *capitulation in British history.*'

The next emergency came at 10.30 on 17 June when it was decided he had to go to America that very day. The Prime Minister's train pulled out of Euston at 12.15 and arrived in Stranraer at 22.30 hours. Take-off, from Stranraer Loch, was in a Boeing Clipper flying-boat. Rising above the cloud at 5,000 feet at 00.30 on the 18th they headed into an intense blood-red sky towards the setting Sun. In the morning they over-flew the new Gander Airport in Newfoundland, and continued over a foggy Cape Breton Island, to emerge from bumpy cloud at Cape Cod. They landed on the Potomac River,

Washington, after a continuous flight of 26.5 hours.

Sir Alan Brooke and Sir Charles Wilson heard Winston humming, singing and whistling: 'We're here because we're here.' He had asked the King to send for Anthony Eden, the Foreign Secretary, in the event of his death.

Winston received the previous day's bad news from the Middle East, of Rommel's advance towards Egypt, when he was with the President in the White House on the afternoon of 21 June.

Roosevelt promised delivery of some of the first Sherman tanks. Winston presented his reasons to George Marshall and Harry Hopkins for postponing plans for opening a Second Front. On the 24th he watched a battalion of paratroops dropping into live-firing ranges in South Carolina. He arrived back in his Washington hotel at 19.00 hours and worked through the night, with his secretary, until 03.45. The return home, also by flying-boat touched down at 05.00 hours on the 27th, on the water at Stranraer.

On 1 August, Winston was off again, disguised in a grey beard, to meet Stalin in Astrakhan. Air Marshal Portal borrowed an American B24 Liberator (named *Commando*) for completion of this visit to Gibraltar, Cairo, Teheran and Moscow. It was still painted with stars and stripes rather than RAF roundels. Discussions in Cairo centred on future command of the 8th Army (General Bernard Montgomery) with Brooke making it clear that all operations in the Middle East depended upon a continuing supply of oil from Abadan. The party flew on 5 August to Burg el Arab at dawn and drove to El Alamein. They left Heliopolis

Winston in Cairo, August 1942, with the South African Prime Minister, Field-Marshal Jan Smuts

Aerodrome at 02.00 hours on the 11th for Teheran.

The following morning, at 06.45, they took off for Moscow. Stalin regarded the refusal of the Allies to open a Second Front as showing deficiencies in courage and resolve rather than restraint due to lack of resources. Brooke failed to get Russian co-operation for joint defence of the Caucasus and the vulnerable approaches to Middle East oil which the Germans never tested. Winston's final vodka-filled fling with Stalin lasted from 19.00 on the 15th to 03.00 the following morning. The Russian dictator obtained a promise from the Prime Minister that he would press for an Allied invasion of northern Norway in January (despite this being the month already scheduled for an attack on North Africa).

Later that night, at 05.30 hours, the four Liberators lifted off from Moscow Aerodrome for a 9.5-hour flight to Teheran. On the 17th they returned to Cairo, braced for Rommel's expected offensive, and took off after sandstorms on the 23rd. The aircraft refuelled at Gibraltar and proceeded to Lyneham, Wiltshire, from where the VIP party were driven to Swindon, for a special train which arrived at Paddington at 23.15 hours on the 24th. Much to his own disappointment, Brooke had felt compelled to turn down Winston's offer of the 8th Army command that went to Montgomery, because it would take months for his replacement as Chief of the Imperial General Staff to master the complexities of restraining the Prime Minister's impulsive nature.

They were relaxed together, as Brooke recorded in his diary: 'This forged one more link between him and me! He is the most difficult man I have ever served with, but thank God for having given me the opportunity of trying to serve such a man in a crisis such as the one the country is going through at present.'

The great news from the western desert came initially in a decrypted Enigma intercept in which Hitler told Rommel's Afrika Korps to choose between 'death and victory' as Montgomery broke out from Alamein. This was followed by Allied landings in Casablanca, Oran and Algiers. Winston ordered the ringing of church bells across the land in celebration. Montgomery was rewarded with a knighthood. Saving Egypt was the turning point of the war, Winston said in a speech at the Mansion House, on 10 November:

> 'This is not the end. It is not even the beginning of the end. But it is the end of the beginning.' Winston's Mansion House speech on 10 November 1942

The Chiefs of Staff then had to dissuade Winston from demanding an invasion of France in 1943, whilst keeping open options for amphibious landings in the Mediterranean, with a view to forcing Italy out of the war.

1943 The war continued to turn against the Germans in Russia and North Africa and the Japanese were held on the doorstep to India and in sight of Australia. President Roosevelt arranged to meet Winston in Casablanca, Morocco, on 14 January for joint military and political planning of future strategy. Winston went to Marrakesh, on the 24th, to see the President off in his plane and spend a couple of days painting.

Typically, the following day, he decided to send for the pilots to fly to Egypt. They crossed the Atlas Mountains in the

Unity beside the Heel Stone at Stonehenge - Australian Minister Richard Gardiner Casey, head of the United States Army General George C. Marshall and Prime Minister Winston Churchill

sunset and then 2,300 miles of desert in darkness. Twelve hours later the two parties were re-united for breakfast in the British Embassy in Cairo with Winston 'as fresh as paint', downing white wine after introductory double whiskies and two cigars. They flew on to Siwa Oasis on the 28th and to Adna on the 30th to meet the Turkish leaders over an hilarious dinner conducted in Winston's 'astounding French' which was largely incomprehensible.

Negotiations successfully ensured continued neutrality from the Turks with a pro-Allied bias. The British party went on to Cyprus and Cairo, and then on 3 February to Montgomery's headquarters, in Tripoli. General Bernard Freyberg arranged a march-past of the entire New Zealand Division. The sight of these bronzed and blooded warriors had Winston shedding tears of pride and relief as he realised that victory was now possible.

On the 5th the visitors shifted to Algiers, to meet General Dwight D. Eisenhower - promising him an additional British infantry division - and from there back to Lyneham (landing at 22.30 hours on the 7th after a journey of 10,200 miles).

Roosevelt and Churchill at the press conference following the US-British talks at Casablanca, Morocco, January 1943

After the Cabinet meeting on the 29th, Winston invited Brooke to dinner for a tête-à-tête till after midnight in which he planned their next trip to North Africa and said they should be capturing Greece at the same time as taking Italy. Logistical concerns that springtime centred on maintaining shipping levels across the Atlantic, into the Mediterranean, and out to India, whilst the Americans put their prime resources into running a second war across the Pacific.

> *'There is no finer investment for any community than putting milk into babies.'* Winston in a wireless broadcast on 21 March 1943

On 19 April a display was put on for Winston at Hatfield Aerodrome to introduce him to the future - a prototype jet fighter - after which he held a Cabinet meeting and discussed plans to attack Tunis and recapture Burma, till one o'clock in the morning. He set about arranging an emergency visit of strategy planners to Washington, leaving Greenock on the troopship RMS *Queen Mary* at 17.30 on 5 May (along with 3,000 troops). Escorts through the U-boat belt included an aircraft carrier, cruiser and a Sunderland flying-boat. Approaching New York, they were shadowed by two American cruisers, four destroyers, and a Catalina flying-boat, and anchored in the mist on the 11th.

The reception in Washington, at 18.30 hours that day, was hosted by the President. Winston and Brooke were ecstatic when, alone with Roosevelt on the 12th, they received news of the surrender of Tobruk. A total of a quarter of a million Germans had been taken prisoner. The Americans, however, wanted more, and failed to understand that lack of resources prevented advances into Burma or a quick return to France.

To them, the Mediterranean was a diversion, and the Pacific remained the first thing on their mind. Winston complicated things by also wanting landings in the Balkans and Norway. The eventual agreement was to continue the war against Italy whilst shipping more American and Canadian men and supplies across the Atlantic so that 29 divisions could invade France in 1944.

The party flew home on 26 May in the Clipper flying-boat *Bristol*, in a 17-hour flight of 3,260 miles at 7,000 feet, via Botwood in Newfoundland, to Gibraltar. An alarming experience of two bangs and a flash were caused by lightning hitting the bows. On 28 May they continued to Algiers to update Eisenhower on the Washington Conference. Winston delivered a speech from the Roman amphitheatre at Carthage.

> *'Yes, I was speaking where the cries of Christian virgins rent the air whilst roaring lions devoured them, and yet I am no lion and am certainly not a virgin.'* Winston speaking in the Roman amphitheatre at Carthage

Montgomery was briefed on 3 June and the following day the party returned to Gibraltar in Winston's York airliner (after 2,250 miles around the Mediterranean). They landed at Northolt (1,400 miles) at 18.00 hours on the 5th. Winston chaired a conference on 29 June to discuss the development of the German V2 rocket and the need for bombing Peenemunde experimental station. On 5 August Winston was off again to America, sailing from the Clyde in a newly-repainted RMS *Queen Mary*. On the 9th she docked in Halifax and the visitors boarded a train to the St Lawrence River where Winston was met by Canadian Premier Mackenzie King and taken by road to Quebec.

The Tube Alloy project provided cover for deadly serious science. Cambridge physicists had decamped to Montreal to develop an atomic bomb. There was also a diversion into 'funny science' with Winston having unwittingly provided a humorous aside to incessant discussion of war plans. He promoted a Heath-Robinson project devised by 'mad professor' Geoffrey

Roosevelt and Churchill at the Teheran Conference, November 1943, with General Sir Alan Brooke (Chief of Imperial General Staff) and Sir Andrew Cunningham (Admiral of the Fleet)

Pyke who invented a form of frozen wood-pulp to turn icebergs into floating airfields. Lord Louis Mountbatten, head of South East Asia Command, tested the concept by firing a revolver into a lump of Pykrete (which survived that assault but failed on questions of practicality and scale).

Winston went on to Washington on 1 September. He returned to Halifax on the 12th, overnight, to board HMS *Renown* with the claim that the war against the submarines was being won.

> 'If they attack the convoys we shall be able to attack the U-boats. With the large number of auxiliary aircraft carriers [escort carriers] now coming into service we are able to give a measure of air protection to convoys and to conduct an aggressive warfare against U-boats in those areas which are beyond the reach even of long-range aircraft.'
> Winston on the Battle of the Atlantic

Winston's daughter Mary was nearly washed over the side on her 21st birthday when the battle-cruiser made a sudden zig-zag manoeuvre at 29 knots to counter possible torpedo attack. They sailed into Greenock to a rapturous reception on the 19th. On 3 November, Winston hosted a Downing Street dinner for the King, who did not leave until 12.30 am. Buckingham Palace returned the honour on the 10th. By the 15th, Winston was off again in *Renown*, from Plymouth to Gibraltar. Captain Richard Pim's map-room staff worked out that the Prime Minister had so far travelled 111,000 miles on his wartime missions, including 792 hours at sea and 339 hours in the air.

They went on to Algiers, Malta and Alexandria where President Roosevelt came ashore from the new battleship USS *Iowa* for the five-day Allied conference at Mena House on 22 November. Winston took off in the York for Teheran on the 27th. Stalin was relieved to hear that there would be Allied landings in southern France (leaving him a free hand in the Balkans) and agreed for the Overlord invasion of Normandy to be postponed from 1 May to 1 June 1944.

Stalin reserved the right to dismember Germany -

receiving backing from Roosevelt for splitting it into zones - and to determine the future of Poland and Finland. The Russian leader half-joked that he wanted to see the leading 50,000 German officers and technicians shot dead as a preventive measure against future aggression. During these discussions Winston had emphasised the need for deception and duplicity:

> *'In war the truth must be accompanied by an escort of lies to ensure its security.'*
> Winston to Sir Alan Brooke

When his birthday was celebrated, at a banquet on 30 November, there were 69 candles burning on the cake. England was going pink, he joked, which as Stalin observed was 'a sign of good health'. Politically, however, the Prime Minister felt sidelined, and he was succumbing to a cold. He flew by C54 Skymaster - a gift from the President - from Teheran to Cairo on 2 December. Roosevelt reluctantly agreed to cancel Operation Buccaneer, the proposed assault on the Japanese-held Andaman Islands in the Indian Ocean, as it would need too many men and ships.

On the 11th Winston flew to Tunis to meet Eisenhower in his villa at Carthage but ended up staying there in bed critically ill with pneumonia. He did not get up till Christmas Day, when he emerged for a conference on the Anzio landings, wearing his siren suit and a pair of bedroom slippers embossed with his initials in gold letters. By the end of the year he had flown on to Marrakesh to stay at the Villa Taylor and relax with his easel.

1944 Winston's Moroccan sojourn ended on 14 January when he flew to Gibraltar where the battleship HMS *King George V* and cruiser HMS *Mauritius* were waiting to take him to England. They sailed for Plymouth on the 15th and docked in the rain on the night of the 17th.

Winston's special train arrived in Paddington at 10.00 hours the following morning. By 11.30 he was standing at the despatch box in the House of Commons for question time. The 12.15 Cabinet meeting updated him on the V1 flying-bomb

General Sir Alan Brooke with Winston in Normandy, visiting General Sir Bernard Montgomery (right) at his field headquarters near Bayeux, 12 June 1944

offensive. Winston's cavalier disregard for names had its apotheosis in confusion of the sort that any of us might make over dinner on 9 February. Three Berlins were involved. Thinking he was talking to philosopher Isiah Berlin, he put a series of challenging intellectual questions to puzzled songwriter Irving Berlin, whilst having in mind the 'Big City' on the far side of Germany.

Alcohol and a punishing regime caused self-doubt over the conduct of the war. What happened to the raid on Nuremberg on the night of 30 March led to the accusation of a deliberate leak by MI5 to the Luftwaffe so a double-agent could establish his credentials for the vital invasion-plan deception of Operation Fortitude. The British lost 105 bombers and the Germans just five fighters (an RAF 10.5 per cent loss rate compared with a 3.5 per cent norm).

> *'I am not at all sure that I shall be held to have done very well.'* - Winston to Bob Boothby MP

Winston attended Montgomery's final day-long briefing for Operation Overlord at his St Paul's School headquarters on 15 May. A total of 176,000 men and 20,000 vehicles were to take part in the biggest armada in history.

Admiral Sir Bertram Ramsay, the Allied Naval

Commander, reluctantly agreed to a request from Winston to witness the D-Day landings. He arranged for the Prime Minister to sail in HMS *Belfast*, from Weymouth Bay, on D-Minus 1. The Chiefs of Staff were horrified and did their best to block the plan. Winston persisted, however, and was only dissuaded by the King himself, who pointed out that he too wanted to go but had agreed to stop at home.

In the event the invasion was postponed by 24 hours, to enable an Atlantic depression to blow through, and took place on the morning of Tuesday 6 June. Five beach-heads were established in Normandy, at a cost of 4,572 lives, more than half of them American on closely-fought Omaha Beach. Winston remained determined to cross at the earliest opportunity, and sailed from Portsmouth in the destroyer HMS *Kelvin* for a day-trip on the 12th. He was met by General Sir Bernard Montgomery, commander of 21st Army Group, with a convoy of jeeps which took them towards Bayeux. Winston was surprised at the healthy state of the countryside after four years of occupation.

> 'We are surrounded by fat cattle lying in luscious pastures with their paws crossed!' - Winston in liberated France

Field-Marshal Sir Alan Brooke commented: 'The French population did not seem in any way pleased to see us arrive as a victorious country to liberate France. They had been quite content as they were, and we were bringing war and desolation to the country.'

That night the first V1 'doodle-bug' flying-bombs fell on London, blocking railway lines into Liverpool Street Station, and much bigger rockets were expected at any time (the first V2 hit Chiswick on 8 September).

Winston returned to France, to American Utah Beach and the British Mulberry Harbour at Arromanches, on 20 July, and attempted to fly back to Cherbourg a fortnight later. The weather deteriorated, however, and they had difficulty returning to Thorney Island. On 7 August he tried again, and then went in to Italy in mid-August, to meet Marshal Tito of Yugoslavia in the

Villa Rivalta, beside the Bay of Naples. From the destroyer HMS *Kimberley* he watched the Operation Dragoon landings of American troops along the French Riviera.

Winston was reluctant to accept that with Eisenhower firmly across the Channel, Allied forces in Europe were now under United States leadership, and he was no longer the decisive war leader - even in his own land. He was close to exhaustion and a constant source of confusion, frustration and interference to the Chiefs of Staffs as they ran the war. They were often at the receiving end of his 'black dog days' of clinical depression. On the other hand, Winston frequently found President Roosevelt's indecision insufferable, and protested at endless calls for consultation.

> *'Action is paralysed if everybody is to consult everybody else about everything before it is taken.'* Winston to President Roosevelt

On 6 September Winston sailed from the Clyde on the *Queen Mary*, escorted by the cruisers HMS *Berwick* and *Kent*, for a conference in the Frontenac Hotel, Quebec. Arrangements were confirmed for the war in Italy, progress towards the Ruhr, and a projection that the war against Japan would go on for 18 months after that against Germany had ended. He returned to London for the state opening of Parliament on 26 September. Then he was off by air in the York from Northolt, on 8 October, to Naples, Cairo and Moscow. Arrival proved doubly hazardous as the undercarriage of the Prime Minister's York was damaged in landing at Cairo and he transferred to Field-Marshal Brooke's aircraft. The undercarriage of this jammed on coming into Moscow. An emergency crank release mechanism had to be used to lower the wheels.

Drink flowed continuously, day and night, between banquets. Stalin pledged Russian help to end the war with Japan but wanted to know what he would get out of it and discussions concluded without the future of Poland being resolved. The Soviet dictator saw off his guests in the rain from Moscow Aerodrome on the 19th. They stopped off at Sarabus, in the Crimea, and landed at Cairo on the 20th. They flew on to Naples in a big curve via Benghazi, to avoid passing near German-occupied Crete, and then across southern and western France, to arrive at Northolt - after covering 10,500 miles - on the 22nd.

On 10 November Winston hosted a dinner at the Quai d'Orsay in Paris, reflecting that the last time he was there, in 1940, the French were burning their archives on abandoning the city. The following day, with General de Gaulle, he passed through the Arc de Triomphe to continuous cries of 'Churcheel, Churcheel'. The year ended with German General Rundstedt mounting a last offensive through the snowy forests of the Ardennes, the Italian campaign stagnating, and Winston setting off from Northolt in the Skymaster, to spend Christmas in Greece, resisting a communist take-over, from the cruiser HMS *Ajax*.

Official portrait of the Big Three - Churchill, Roosevelt and Stalin - at the Yalta Conference in the Crimea, February 1945

> 'Why didn't they fight the Germans like they are fighting us now?' - Winston on the Greek partisans

1945 On 3 January, Winston flew from Northolt to Paris, to meet Eisenhower and de Gaulle in Versailles. On the 5th he was at Montgomery's headquarters - after Monty claimed to have saved the Americans from the Ardennes debacle - and flew back from Brussels to Northolt. The next major trip was to Russia.

Winston arrived by Skymaster in Malta on 30 January, just before dawn, with a temperature which kept him in the aeroplane for the rest of the day and night. He transferred in the afternoon to HMS *Orion* in the Grand Harbour at Valetta.

Wrecked rail bridge at Wesel where Winston withdrew under shell-fire on 25 March 1945

On 2 February he flew 1,400 miles to Saki and was then driven for eight hours through the mountains of the Crimea to Vorontzov Villa, overlooking the Black Sea at Yalta. The British party of more than 30 included 'Eden, Leathers, three Field Marshals, one or two Admirals of the Fleet, a posse of Generals, a number of high civilian officials including Sir Edward Bridges, secretary of the Cabinet.' Stalin attended on the 4th to discuss co-ordination of offensive actions and bombing raids. The Britons left Vorontzov Villa in a snowstorm on the 7th for Sebastopol.

Winston visited the battlefield of Balaclava to look down on the valley floor along which the Light Brigade rode towards the Russian guns. The main British contingent boarded the SS *Franconia* at Sebastopol, for a leisurely voyage to Malta, but Winston decided to drive back to Saki and fly to Athens. On the 19th he flew back to London via Egypt, where he lunched with a placid and frail President Roosevelt aboard the cruiser USS *Quincy*, at Alexandria. He also had talks with King Ibn Saud at Fayoum. Winston, with Brooke and Ismay, flew from Northolt on 2 March in the new Prime Ministerial C54, just after 11.00 hours. Having lunched in Brussels they went in two Dakotas to Eindhoven - to be met by Montgomery - and were taken to operational headquarters at Geldrop, Holland, to stay in General Eisenhower's train. On the 3rd Winston stopped their Rolls-Royce, holding up a column of 30 cars, for the purpose of urinating on the Siegfried Line.

> *'Gentlemen, this is one of the operations connected with this great war which must not be reproduced graphically.'*
> Winston to photographers as he relieved himself on the Siegfried Line

On 4 March, Winston took charge of an 8-inch gun, at Aachen. Having chalked 'For Hitler personally' on a shell he fired it across the Rhine and then went on to Gennep to see the line of Bailey Bridges across the River Meuse. The return from Brussels was shortly before 11.00 on 6 March, in the Skymaster, to return to Northolt just after midday. Winston returned to Montgomery's headquarters at Venlo in a Dakota on 23 March to witness the crossing of the Rhine and entry into the Reich.

That took place on a clear, moonlit night and the following morning at 08.45 Winston and Brooke were at a viewpoint near Xanten watching boats ferrying across the river with a constant stream of aircraft and gliders overhead. On the 25th they crossed the river near Wesel, at a wrecked railway bridge, and only withdrew after German shells began falling only 100 yards upstream. General Simpson of the United States Army insisted they left. Brooke considered that Winston had deliberately put himself in 'the most exposed position possible' and - like Nelson - 'would really have liked to be killed on the front at this moment of success'.

President Roosevelt died in office on 12 April, during his fourth term, and was replaced by Harry Truman. Hitler shot himself at the end of the month. The Italian front surrendered on the 3rd and the German armies in the west surrendered to Field-Marshal Montgomery on Luneburg Heath at 18.30 hours on 4 May. The 8th was designated Victory Europe Day for national celebrations with crowds thronging central London and the War Cabinet and Chiefs of Staff joining the King and Queen for speeches at Buckingham Palace at 16.30 hours. By public demand there were repeat performances from the Home Office balcony in Whitehall.

Princess Elizabeth, Queen Elizabeth, Winston Churchill and King George VI, greeting VE Day crowds from the balcony of Buckingham Palace, 8 May 1945

In the meantime the war against Japan continued, with the Americans unable to make up their minds on encirclement or invasion. The British Chiefs of Staff and Foreign Secretary Anthony Eden began to face the reality that Russia as the new world power was also going to be the probable future enemy. Winston foresaw the 'Russian bear sprawled over Europe'.

Democracy took precedence at home with the return of party politics for a general election. Despite warm welcomes throughout the outdoor electioneering, delivering a misleading message of invincibility - 'Good old Winnie' - his future was hostage to a national determination to revenge Tory failings in the 1930s. His first party political broadcast also backfired when he equated socialism with 'political police' and 'some form of Gestapo'.

Polling day was 5 July but the result remained in the ballot boxes for three weeks whilst the votes of those serving overseas were brought home for counting. On the 15th both the Prime Minister and his deputy and Labour opponent Clement Attlee left for the Potsdam Conference in Berlin, and the final groundwork for German occupation and post-war boundaries. There, on 23 July, Winston received a report on the secret explosion in New Mexico of the atomic bomb, and was sure it would bring an almost immediate Japanese surrender. They returned in the Skymaster from Gatow to Northolt on the 25th.

The bombshell awaiting them was the election result - a Labour landslide - which put Attlee into 10 Downing Street and made Winston the Leader of the Opposition (he had been returned for the Woodford part of former Epping constituency). In August, whilst staying at Claridge's, the Churchills bought 28 Hyde Park Gate as their London home. There was also the distraction of extensive

Victory crowds mobbing Winston and his bodyguard Walter Thompson (looking left) in Victoria Street, Westminster

grounds, waiting to be brought back into cultivation, at Chartwell in Kent.

> *'It is the will of the people. I shall paint for the rest of my days. I've never painted so well before.'* Winston after the 1945 election result

LEADER OF THE OPPOSITION

1946-1950 Being in Opposition, Winston was spared the blame for worsening national austerity. There was political direction of labour and bread and potatoes were rationed. Growing debts and shortages made the recent war seem like a time of opportunity and plenty. Winston always thrived in adversity.

On 5 March 1946, in a speech for President Truman at Fulton, Missouri, he warned of the 'Iron Curtain' coming down across Europe. There were 2,500,000 Russian soldiers in Stalin's satellite states.

> Winston, speaking in Zurich, called for *'. . . a kind of United States of Europe [with] a European army under a unified command in which we would all bear a working and honourable part.'*

Jack Churchill, Winston's younger brother, died from an aneurysm in February 1947. Health was also on Winston's mind and he agreed to have a hernia operation that June. In December he took his paint-box to Marrakesh and worked on his memoirs of *The Second World War*. Independence for India left him observing that the British Empire was dying from within, in 'a hideous act of self-mutilation', rather than being destroyed by outside pressures. In Monte Carlo, while playing cards at 02.00 hours on 24 August 1949, Winston suffered a minor arterial clot.

He recovered sufficiently to be briefed the following month by the Chancellor of the Exchequer, Stafford Cripps, on devaluation of the pound. 'Good old Churchill,' was the cry as he entered Downing Street. He proceeded to bounce back into the full fray of a general election, with speeches and broadcasts across the country, in February 1950. Attlee scraped home, however, but there would soon be another election.

PRIME MINISTER ONCE AGAIN

1951-1955 The general election of October 1951 did not turn into the expected anti-Labour landslide but it was a positive and workable result - the Conservative majority over all other parties was 18. The King asked Winston to form a government. To their surprise, Winston and Foreign Secretary Anthony Eden found that the Labour Government had spent millions on developing atomic weapons without telling Parliament or the party, having hid expenditure by spreading its accountancy across numerous departmental budgets. At the end of the year Winston and Eden sailed to the United States in the *Queen Mary*. Winston was given the honour of addressing Congress.

The Prime Minister was showing inevitable signs of ageing, principally deafness and a waddle in his walking, but for King George VI the prognosis was much bleaker. He had a secret operation for lung cancer which was found to be terminal. On 31 January 1952, Winston stood with the King and Queen, in sub-zero conditions on the tarmac at London Airport, to wave goodbye to Princess Elizabeth and the Duke of Edinburgh as they departed for a tour of East Africa, Australia and New Zealand. The King suggested taking a nip of whisky. Churchill replied that he had already done so:

> *'When I was younger I made it a rule never to take strong drink before lunch. It is now my rule never to do so before breakfast.'*
> Winston to King George VI

In the early hours of 5 February the King died in his sleep at Sandringham. Without knowing it at the time, Princess Elizabeth became Queen Elizabeth II - also in her sleep - on safari in the Treetops Hotel in Kenya. The day's Cabinet meeting was cancelled and the Queen returned to England. On 7 March she made Winston Churchill a Knight of the Garter. His other accolade of the year was Alfred Nobel's Prize for Literature though it was awarded for biographical work rather than recognising the mastery of words that changed the history of the world. He had marshalled and mobilised the English language as a weapon of war.

In June, Winston suffered a stroke, but continued to chair Cabinet meetings, appeared in public at the St Leger in Doncaster and recuperated in Monte Carlo. The next major hurdles were a credible speech at Margate in October and a masterly appraisal on the state of the nation to the House of Commons on 3 November. One concession for his health was to trade-down from Cuban cigars to mild Filipinos though normal brandies and whiskies were maintained.

Winston's memory for names was failing. This was not helped by his habit of satirising them. In Downing Street, his secretary Sir John Colville recalled, Winston referred to Cabinet probationary Deputy Secretary Sir Thomas Padmore as 'Potsdam'. The equally unimpressive General Sir Nevil Brownjohn was 'that fellow Shorthorn'.

The BOAC Strato-cruiser *Canopus,* which had just taken the Queen to Bermuda in November 1953, picked up the Prime Minister and his delegation from Heathrow on 1 December, to return to the island for the international Bermuda Conference. President Eisenhower wanted an Allied response to the intractable problem of the growing number of Soviet nuclear weapons. Winston was frustrated that everything had to be translated into French - regarding the presence of the French Prime Minister as irrelevant - and became increasingly tired.

> *'The world is in an awful state, I cannot cope with it.'* - Winston to Lord Moran in Bermuda.

Fearing another stroke, Winston told Lord Moran on 19 March 1954 that he would resign in June. He withstood an hour of hostile interruptions in an acrimonious Parliamentary debate on the hydrogen bomb on 5 April. Later in the month he persuaded the Cabinet to refuse an American request to help the French after their defeat at Dien Bien Phu in the jungle of Indo-China.

Since the coronation, television fever had gripped the nation, and five million homes now had sets though the only service was from the BBC. Legislation went through Parliament to establish commercial television (its debut being on Thursday 22 September 1955, though initially only to 200,000 homes).

After resigning as Prime Minister, Winston resumed his pre-war seat below the gangway beside the Treasury Bench. His statue was unveiled in the Guildhall on 21 June (standing between Nelson and Wellington). He gave a speech expressing the hope that humanity would not destroy itself. The statue pleased him as much as Graham Sutherland's portrait had appalled Clemmie (causing her to cut it up and put it on the bonfire).

RETIRED STATESMAN

1956-1964 Winston delighted in Chartwell but Clemmie preferred staying in Hyde Park Gate and playing bezique. They settled on moving to France - 'semi-permanently' - on 11 January 1956 but returned in a month. On

Winston the painter in his orchard studio at Chartwell

29 February, Winston voted in Westminster, in a defence debate. From then on they moved in a triangle between France, Chartwell and London.

It was a rejuvenated Winston who appeared as guest of honour at Prime Minister Anthony Eden's Downing Street dinner for Soviet leaders Bulganin and Khrushchev in April 1956. The following month he was invited to visit Germany and awarded the Charlemagne Prize. He delivered a speech about a united Europe in which he predicted that German re-unification would come about when the strength of western forces became so strong that Russia had to accept the inevitable. Winston thought he might have retired prematurely but reconsidered the notion as the Suez crisis destroyed Sir Anthony Eden's career. He declined the suggestion that he should speak in the House; his instincts were to stand firm on the Suez Canal.

In France in October 1956 a 'cerebral spasm' left him partially paralysed. Mentally, however, he was still astute, correctly predicting that Harold Macmillan would take over from Eden. The Queen invited Winston to the Palace on 9 January 1957 to confirm the news.

In February 1958, Winston suffered a bout of broncho-pneumonia in Nice after lunching with Ari Onassis and playing chemin-de-fer on his yacht at Monte Carlo. Back at Chartwell, in April, he had recovered quite well but friends such as Jock Colville and his doctor, Lord Moran, heard that the Queen had asked Downing Street to sort out Winston's funeral arrangements.

Winston initially wanted to be buried at Chartwell but on reflection opted to be beside his father at Bladon, near Woodstock. Concern, however, was premature. At the bidding of Harold Macmillan, Winston the politician made a speech in his Woodford constituency for the April 1959 general election. Winston the Anglo-American went to Washington in May. Winston the painter mounted a one-man show at the Royal Academy.

In 1960 he was back in *Christina*, the Onassis yacht, at Martinique. Throughout his closing years he played the part that was ingrained in the national psyche - the signature cigar and V-sign for Victory, with a scowl of defiance that warmed into an old man's smile, whether emerging from a siren suit or a blanket. To pollsters the British public would proclaim him the greatest Englishman who had ever lived. He did not stand down as MP until 1964.

STATE FUNERAL

1965 Winston died after his third stroke, at 28 Hyde Park Gate, on 25 January 1965. Members of his family at the bedside included Lady Churchill, his son Randolph, and two daughters Mrs Mary Soames and Miss Sarah Churchill. He lay in state at Westminster Hall, in a coffin draped with the Union Flag, on which rested the insignia of the Knight of the Garter. Tens of thousands of people filed past the catafalque, in a mile-long queue led by the Prime Minister, Harold Wilson, with Mrs Wilson.

> *'Shortly after 8 a.m. this morning, Sunday January 24th, Sir Winston Churchill died at his London home.'* [signed] Moran

Winston was given the first State funeral for a commoner since that of Gladstone in 1898. After the service in St Paul's Cathedral, on 30 January, the coffin was taken to Waterloo Station. A special train, hauled by Battle of Britain class locomotive *Sir Winston Churchill*, made the final journey to Oxfordshire, for interment beside his parents in Bladon churchyard.

The other Churchill shrine, given to the National Trust with 79 acres of parkland in 1946, is Chartwell, near Westerham, Kent. Winston had a marmalade cat called Jock and insisted there should always be one at Chartwell. Jock III, the third incarnation, featured in *Your Cat* magazine in 1998. Current cat Jock IV does not do public relations and shuns the visitors.

> *'The greater part of this wall was built between the years 1925 & 1932 by Winston with his own hands.'* Chartwell inscription